A DESCRIPTION

OF

HOWE'S CAVE;

WITH A POPULAR TREATISE ON THE

FORMATION OF CAVES IN LIME ROCK,

FROM THE SIZE OF A QUILL TO A MAMMOTH.

Illustrated with Numerous Engravings.

ALBANY:
WEED, PARSONS AND COMPANY, PRINTERS.
1865.

A DESCRIPTION

OF

HOWE'S CAVE;

WITH A POPULAR TREATISE ON THE

FORMATION OF CAVES IN LIME ROCK,

FROM THE SIZE OF A QUILL TO A MAMMOTH.

Illustrated with Numerous Engravings.

ALBANY:
WEED, PARSONS AND COMPANY, PRINTERS.
1865.

HOWE'S CAVE.

Caves are found in various portions of the world and in various kinds of rock, but lime rock is their choice seat, and contain more than all other formations in the world.

The primary limestone formations contain the largest number of caves, but they are limited in extent by the limited extent of the rock in which they are found, while the largest caves are found in lime rock of a much larger extent and of a more recent geological date.

Having now glanced at the rock in which the largest and most numerous caves are found, let us now look at the tools or agents with which nature performs her work, and see how from such simple means such wonderful results are produced.

The direct and indispensable agent employed is water, and the incidental are sand or gravel which operate by mechanical action, which consists in wearing away the rock with which it comes in contact in passing along the channel; but when water has absorbed carbonic acid from the atmosphere or other sources, then another action is added, which is chemical action, which consists in absorbing a small portion of the lime rock with which it comes in contact, and carrying it off in its passage.

The chemical action may operate with equal or greater rapidity upon the hardest rock, while the reverse is true of mechanical action.

Having now briefly examined the tools with which nature works in the formations of caves, let us examine the manner in which they are used, and see how, from two agents, water and sand, and two actions incidental to those agents, mechanical and chemical, caves, stalactites and stalagmites, which assume ten thousand different ludicrous and indescribable forms, are produced, and trace them in their growth from their embryonic state through their different periods of existence to their decay.

The first and absolutely indispensable agent is water, which first operates by finding a passage between some strata of rock or through some crevice, and having found a passage, its own mechanical action begins, and if it contain carbonic acid, then in addition to the mechanical action is the chemical action of the water.

When the passage of the first drop of water is effected the existence of the cave in embryo has commenced, and although it may require innumerable centuries to enlarge it to the size of the quill with which you write, the continued action of the same agent, with the addition of sand and gravel as the cave enlarges, will develope a cave of magnificent dimensions and give to it a thousand curious arches and notches and nooks and conical cavities of almost every conceivable size and form.

When water trickles down from a crevice above into the cave, the water, either by chemical or mechanical action, slowly carries off the rock with which it comes in contact, thus producing cavities varying in size from the slightest perceptible depression to those high conical chambers whose height is yet to be measured.

But this is not all; the water and detritus falling from above may, by its own mechanical action, wear away the rock upon which it falls and form a cavity on the floor of the cave beneath; but, in addition to this, if the falling water is not fully saturated with lime rock before it falls, its chemical action will again be brought into play and the rock removed with increased rapidity; and these cavities, like those formed above, vary in size from the slightest perceptible depression to those of an immense depth.

When the water trickles down the sides of the cave, it forms niches, some of which resemble those in the Capitol at Washington made for the deposit of statuary. In this manner cavities in the sides of the cave are often made of almost every conceivable shape and size.

But sometimes exactly the reverse of this takes place, and instead of a cavity being formed in the top of the cave, a pendulous material is formed, pointing down like an icicle, and instead of a cavity being formed below, a mass is formed extending upward; and this leads us to the subject of stalactites and stalagmites, and first, incidentally, to the ornaments formed by them.

Nature having now formed the cavern with its thousand curious curves and windings, and niches above and below and on the walls, with its music halls and museum departments, with its Harlem tunnels and haunted castles, with its winding ways and rotundas, with running streams and stygian lakes, has as yet only prepared it for the reception of her finer artistic work.

In architecture it is yet to be stored with columns, arches and gargoyles, and a thousand other things.

In sculpture, the niches are to be filled with statues of every size and form, and clothed in the habiliments of nudity, and the waters with mermaids and other appropriate designs.

In music, the rooms are to be hung with the harp and the lyre.

The museum department is yet to become the abode of wild animals whose bones are yet to be incased in marble, and perhaps to be exhumed to fill some museum by races of men whose progenitors are not yet denizens of earth.

The rooms are yet to be filled with drapery and things bearing a strong resemblance to household furniture.

The menagerie is yet to be painted upon the walls, and a thousand other things too numerous to mention, all of which is done by the action of water.

We have seen that water holding carbonic acid has acquired the property of dissolving a small portion of lime rock, with which it comes in contact, and carrying it off in its passage.

We have now to examine the process by which this same water, instead of carrying off its lime rock, is made to deposit it upon the part with which it comes in contact.

When a drop of water charged with lime rock to its point of saturation hangs on the arch of the cave, a small portion evaporates and deposits just the amount of lime rock held in the water evaporated; but if the water is not fully saturated with lime rock no deposit takes place till the point of saturation is reached, and it is by a continuation of this process for long periods of time that pendulous masses hanging from the arch of the cave are formed, called stalactites, but when the water collects faster than it evaporates, it falls off on the floor beneath, which, by slowly evaporating, deposits its lime rock, thus forming a material extending upwards called a stalagmite. When these extend so as to meet, they form pillars, and sometimes columns.

When several of these stalactites and stalagmites form within a few inches of each other, they often extend in length and size so as to unite and form a large column.

When the water drips over some jetting rock it forms sheets and valances, and a thousand strangely shaped forms.

When the cave is partly filled with clay, and the falling water deposits its lime rock on its surface, it forms a covering of variable thickness, and when the clay on which it was deposited is washed away, it forms a bridge spanning the cave from side to side.

When the material of which these stalactites are formed is pure, the stalactites are white and often translucent, but when the water from which they are deposited contains impurities, the color varies from a white to a dark brown, and frequently the color varies in the same stalactite, in layers or concentric rings, the number of which may be greatly increased by the microscope, thus, perhaps, recording the wet and dry seasons of the year ages ago.

Small stalactites resemble icicles, except in being hollow

several inches from the lower end, which is caused by the evaporation of the water from the outside of the drop, which hangs from its lower end, thus causing a deposit of stalactite where the evaporation takes place, and thus forms a tube. They continue to increase in size by the evaporation of the water which runs down the outside, and the larger the surface exposed the more rapidly is the water evaporated and the material deposited.

Stalagmites, unlike stalactites, are never hollow, and are generally more blunt.

Stalagmites vary in size from a small icicle to a haystack, and sometimes completely obstruct the passage in the cave.

The rapidity with which these stalactite formations are produced depends upon the extent to which the water is charged with lime rock, and the rapidity with which it is evaporated.

Having now seen how stalactitic formations are produced, let us now see how the same agent which gave them birth and growth again assumes its prerogative and denies their title to the land of their nativity, a title which they seem to have acquired by prescriptive right for unknown ages.

When water holding carbonic acid, which is not completely saturated with lime rock, comes in contact with stalactitic formations, it absorbs the stalactite and removes it in its passage, precisely in the same manner as the rock of which it was formed was removed.

Hitherto only two agents (water and sand), and two actions incidental to those agents (mechanical and chemical), have played a part in the drama.

Let us now examine the effect of gravitation (perhaps hastened by earthquakes), and see how large rooms are formed, mountains raised and destroyed, side passages or new caverns brought into existence, sink-holes in the earth are made, and death or decay of the old cave accomplished.

Coeval with the development of the larger rooms is the beginning of decay, the formation of mountains and the commencement of new caves.

Sometimes earthquakes or other causes separate an immense mass of rock from the arch of the cave, which falls and forms a nearly corresponding elevation on the floor beneath, and this is the first great step toward decay. This fallen mass of rock may, after a long time, be reduced in size, or even removed by the stream flowing over its summit or through its base, thus altering the relation of the arch above to the mountain below.

Thus large rooms are formed which, though often of irregular shape, are well calculated to excite wonder and amazement.

The next result which follows from the fallen mass of rock, is the obstruction afforded to the stream, which, if complete, begins at once to hunt some passage around the mountain, between some strata or through some crevice, and form a side passage or cave which may enter the main cave many rods below, or, like some strange comet, acknowledge no law but its own, and pursue its course, by virtue of its own prerogative, to parts unknown.

When the fallen mass of rock only obstructs the passage of water during the floods of spring, the boring of the cave will continue only for a few weeks in the year, but, perhaps, before the new cave has reached its period of childhood, the fallen mass is removed, and the growth of the cave suspended for an eternal age, which means only till another mass of rock falls, perhaps from the same place, and again compels the water to resume its labor and bore out the rock slowly and, perhaps, interruptedly, till it rivals the old cave in size and magnificence, and which, in its turn, is to meet with similar obstructions, and rear another brood of young caverns.

It is by a repetition of the fallen mass of rock that so weakens the arch of the cave, that the surface of the ground falls in and forms tunnel shaped holes called sink-holes, which always mark the course and extent of caves whose glory has departed.

Having now briefly glanced at some of the most important items in relation to caves in lime rock, let us now proceed to examine one of nature's most wonderful freaks, known as HOWE'S CAVE, which in its present traversable extent is second to one only in the United States.

HOWE'S CAVE is situated in the town of Cobleskill, county of Schoharie, New York, thirty-eight miles from Albany, immediately on the line of the Albany and Susquehanna Railroad.

It was a knowledge of the kind of rock in which large caves are found. and the sink-holes which mark the track of old caves, together with a general knowledge of the country around that led LESTER HOWE to suppose the country to be cavernous. Thus stimulated by the light of science, he was led to search the country for caves, which he commenced in the spring of 1841, and, after a diligent search, his efforts were crowned with success on the 22d of May, 1842, by the discovery of one of the most extensive and interesting caves in the world, and which now bears his name.

Although nature had formed the cave countless centuries ago, she had also almost completely closed it for the first three-fourths of a mile with clay, gravel, rocks, &c., the largest part of which was done by the action of water alone. To remove this obstruction by the pick, shovel and barrow would be the work of an age. But HOWE, whose capital consisted principally in genius, energy and perseverance, only used the pick, drill and barrow to loosen the obstructions, and then closed the side water passages above, thus causing the water to again resume its labor and remove from the cave the same material it had so rudely deposited ages ago, and reveal to man for the first time this great subterranean passage, where for unknown ages nature and nature's work lay hid in night.

The hill into which the Cave passes, fronts nearly to the southeast, and rises by perpendicular heights, terraces and steep inclined planes to the height of about ninety feet in about the same distance.

The main Cave, as far as it has been explored, is almost wholly embraced by two strata of lime rock, its lower portion passing through a strata of cement or water lime rock, and the upper portion through a strata of pentamerous lime rock. In a few places the upper portion of the Cave just passes through the pentamerous lime rock into the delthyrus strata.

The majority of the branch or side caves are in the same strata as the lower portion of the main Cave, but several of the branch caves are wholly in the pentamerous strata and only a few in the delthyrus strata.

The direction of the main Cave varies from north to northwest, but the branches pass in all directions.

The strata through which the Cave passes, dips slightly to the south.

The water always flows towards the entrance of the main cave, but the whole of it is discharged by the side passages except during the high water of spring.

High water is seldom sustained more than a day or two at a time, except during the floods of spring.

Almost the whole of the water is furnished by caverns which are now too much filled with gravel to follow for a long distance, but that it passes through caves for many miles, is evident as the cold water of spring is raised to the temperature of 48 fh. before it reaches the traversable portion of the Cave.

The temperature of the air is said to be uniformly at 48 fh. at the distance of half a mile from the entrance at all times of the year.

One interesting phenomenon connected with this Cave is the strong currents of air which blow in different directions at different times, and which is subject to annual and often to diurnal changes.

During the warm season of the year, when the temperature out of the Cave is higher than within, the current blows out, but during the cold season when the air out of the Cave is colder than within, the current blows into the Cave, and the rule which applies to seasons of the year also govern the daily changes of the wind in the Cave.

It is by this natural to and fro current of wind that the air in the Cave is always fresh and wholesome.

The best time for visiting the Cave is from May till October and from December till February.

Generally, within these periods, the visitor may pass over three miles and return without being wet by a drop of water. It may, also, be frequently visited at other times of the year with but little inconvenience from water.

Having now obtained some general ideas of HOWE'S CAVE, let us now prepare for a visit; and, first, the gentlemen are furnished with a pair of overalls, a loose coat and a hat, and the ladies with pants, a bloomer coat, shoes and hat, and all with lamps so hung in gimbals that when we are lost in amazement and silent rapture and the lamps forgotten, they will still stand upright.

Being now equipped according to the law of custom and convenience, let us now pass down two or three flights of stairs in the Cave House to the entrance of the Cave, and think for a moment of passing for miles into the bowels of the earth and hundreds of feet below the forests and fields, where darkness reigns supreme and death to vegetation holds her silent court.

The entrance to HOWE'S CAVE (fig. 1), for the first few rods, is about twelve feet in height, with an averge width of about eight or nine feet. The floor is very even and gently ascending for the first sixty rods or more. After passing about four rods we come to an irregularly shaped notch (fig. 2) on the left, at the further end of which is a cave which varies very much in depth at different years, owing to the amount of gravel deposited or removed by the spring floods. This cave is noted for the immense amount of barytes it formerly furnished for adulteration of whitelead.

Immediately beyond this notch we come to a door D, which is about six feet square and opens directly into

THE SUBTERRANEAN LECTURE ROOM (FIG. 3),

Where the Cave suddenly expands in height from six to ten feet, and in width from six to thirty-five or forty, which continues for about one hundred feet, where it begins to contract, which continues to the entrance of Washington Hall, where it is six feet in height and eight in width. The floor of this room is very flat and even, as is also the top, with the exception of a notch which is about twelve feet wide and eighteen or twenty in height. This notch extends across the Cave on the right, and forms a cave (fig. 4) which extends twenty-five or thirty rods.

This side cave has a few guards in the shape of stalagmites, which give no passes to the corpulent.

This room is sometimes used as a temporary storehouse for the deposit of hydraulic cement which is being hauled from the cave beyond.

But the most remarkable item to be noted in connection with this room, is the occasional appearance of a half-invisible being who styles himself king of this subterranean world, and who ever and anon addresses his alien visitors by some brief discourse pertaining to his dominions.

At one time the following scene occurred: The room contained groups of ladies and gentlemen from almost all parts of the upper world.

Each group with its standard bearer, and each individual with his gimbal lamp in hand, and all wrapped in the habiliments of cave attire, presented at once a scene unique yet strangely enchanting.

Here stood groups of Albanians and Trojans, with their merchants and mechanics and artizans, and near by a group of the Cohosians and others from the regions of the north. Conspicuous in the crowd, are groups from the Empire City and her suburbs, representing almost every department of business.

Conspicuous in the crowd is the standard of the Bostonians, and people from the hundred New England villages.

Suddenly we see a number of standards raise in the groups from the cities and villages of the States of New York and Pennsylvania, each as if to say, we too are here on a visit to your empire.

Here are standards from the Green Isle and their neighbors, even to the continent beyond, and from our own western world we find representatives from Ohio to Oregon and California. Now we see a group from the sunny south, who to evade the sweltering heat peculiar to their clime, have come here where nature seems exhaustless in the variety and grandeur of her works, and where the never changing temperature of this subterranean world fans a cooling breeze to the southerner in summer and a warm breeze to the northerner in winter.

Further in the dim distance we find the Canadian, who, unable to quench his thirst for the wonderful by the world-renowned Falls of Niagara, has come here to obtain his fill.

Amid this scene the king of this subterranean world appeared and addressed the crowd as follows:

My alien friends from all parts of the world above, I always welcome your visits through my dominions. My country, no less than yours, abounds in strange and wonderful things. Whether you look above or below, to the right or to the left, every scene is a page in the natural history of my empire, but whether you are to read a page or a volume is a problem to be solved only by your own close attention and study. Knowledge here, no less than in your world, is the result of self labor and thought, which no babbling pen can supply, and the only possession you can truly and emphatically call your own. Open then your eyes that you may see and understand, and thus obtain the trophies by which you will be surrounded in your journey through every part of my empire. Take them to the land of your domicile and there bear in mind that your torch will shine none the less bright from having lighted your neighbors.

While journeying here, cast a lynx eye upon all things as you pass, and ask how and why.

Do you see my heavens rise in height beyond where light can dart its glimmering ray, ask how came it so.

Or, Alp on Alp ascend beyond where vision's misty rays extend, ask what made it there.

Or, round my mountain in some solid rock or junior cave, ask what office does or has it filled.

Or, in my Harlem tunnel, a line more even, straight and true than ere your boasted GUNTER ever drew, ask how came it so.

Or, in some gorgeous room, where walls are made to echo sound as if from heaven the voices came on mercy's errand down, ask who first designed reflecting walls.

Or, in my stately music rooms, where walls are just so formed that every sound is music, ask where in all nature first the music halls were formed.

Your people of the upper world carried from my empire your first conceptions of habitations, your catacombs and sepulchres, your places of worship and dungeons.

It is here that you first bowed to the shrine of your deity and offered prayers of adoration to the Infinite Being. It is here that your first conceptions of architecture were formed, both in outline and detail. It is here that you first conceived of a pedestal, a base, a shaft, a capital, or an entablature, and countless centuries ere the pendant twigs of your willow marked in outline the gothic arch or the foliage of the acanthus, the volute all were prefigured in my empire.

Boast ye not of antiquity, boast ye not of unborrowed conceptions. Pass on in your journey, and gather gear by every wile that's justified by honor.

Here the crowd passed on to the next department, which is

WASHINGTON HALL (FIG. 5),

Where the cave suddenly expands in height from six to twenty-five feet, and in width from eight to twenty-five feet or more. The arch of this room ascends a little for the first twelve or fifteen rods, where it begins to descend gradually to the Chapel. The floor ascends more rapidly towards the further end of the hall. The sides show decided water-worn marks, almost to the top for nearly the whole length, but this has disappeared; in the top it has now become more rough and uneven, which is just the beginning of the destroying hand of time.

Turning to the right, we ascend about sixteen feet by two flight of stairs, which land us directly in the

BRIDAL CHAMBER (Fig. 6),

Where many a nuptial knot has been tied, including the two daughters of the discoverer.

This chamber is about nine feet in height, sixteen in width, and twenty-five in length. Here, for the first, is seen a few stalactites, which are described by the guides as Washington's epaulet, another as Lady Washington's hood, and another as the statue of Washington, &c.

Near the further end of this room we find, on the right, a double conical cavity or chamber extending upwards to the height of thirty feet, which is partly filled with stalagmite deposit. Just beyond this we come to a door which opens directly into the

WINE ROOM,

Which is about eight feet in height, ten in width, and sixteen in length, and embraces a large stone cistern of clear water, and a store-room for replenishing the stone counter with wine, &c., for the guests of the bridal chamber.

On retracing our steps to the foot of the stairs, we find upon our right a wide cave (fig. 7), which is nearly filled with gravel, which the floods of spring are gradually removing. This cave has been explored only about thirty rods, and contains some very high chambers.

On passing along Washington Hall, we find high clay banks on either side, and are shown some stalactites and their close resemblance to human beings clearly pointed out, all dressed in the habiliments of nudity; one of these is called the Daughter of the Cave. Also some indurated clay formations, which exactly resemble cakes fresh from the baker's oven. Passing along we come to a cave on the right (fig. 8) called the Old Cave, which enters the main cave at fig. 13. It is through this cave that thousands passed annually for three years to the main cave beyond the chapel. Near the entrance of this cave we descend about six feet, where we find a wide cave on the right, which passes under the main cave at fig. 9. This cave is sometimes nearly filled with gravel by the floods of spring, and perhaps the next it is removed.

From the foot of this descent the Old Cave is about three feet high, and from three to six in width, and is smooth and water-worn almost its whole length. The bottom of this cave is broken through in two places into what appears to be caves passing below, and which is now filled with gravel.

There is one place in this cave where the sound of falling water can be distinctly heard by applying the ear close to the bottom, indicating beyond a doubt that a cave and a stream of water passes below.

Retracing our steps to the main cave, we soon come to a cave on the left called the New Cave (fig. 10), which has been recently discovered by the settling of a clay bank. This branch has been explored about twenty rods, and contains some high chambers and bottomless pits. On leaving Washington Hall we come to

THE CHAPEL (Fig. 11).

Here the cave suddenly expands in height from six to forty feet, and in width from six to twenty-five feet or more, and at the distance of about a hundred feet contracts to six or seven feet in height and width. Immediately on entering the Chapel, we ascend some rather steep stone steps to the top of the hill, which is just beyond the center of the room. Here, on looking high over head and to the right, we find a rock of immense size projecting into the Chapel, called by the guides the Rostrum.

Turning now in the direction of the main cave, on looking high into the region of darkness, we see an overhead cave, fig. 12 (indicated by the dotted lines), which is about three feet in diameter, which continues about twenty feet, where it descends six feet, and increases in height to from six to twelve feet. Just at the foot of the descent, we find a cave on the left, c, which is about six feet wide. The main overhead cave passes over the main cave for several rods and then leaves it from the right hand side. At the distance of about thirty rods we find some high conical chambers. The walls of this cave are almost completely covered with stalactite formations. This cave is only accessible by a long ladder, which makes it an undesirable place for the general visitor.

On leaving the chapel, we pass down some steep, rocky steps to the foot of the hill, where we come to

HARLEM TUNNEL (FIG. 14).

Here, on the right, we find the upper end of the old cave (fig. 13). The first portion of this tunnel is a straight, level portion of the cave, which is about twelve feet wide at the bottom, a little narrower at the top, and about seven feet high. This is probably the upper portion of a high cave, the lower portion being filled with clay, stone, &c. After passing a few rods, the visitor is desired to stop while the guides go a long distance in advance to show the straight and even walls of the tunnel, which scarcely varies from a straight line in the distance of nearly thirty rods; but beyond this the walls become more uneven and the top of the cave lower.

On the left side we find a round tube (fig. 15), for the discharge of water through the side of the cave, and a corresponding notch in the top of the cave, which on passing, we come to the next department, which is

CATARACT HALL (FIG. 16),

Which received its name from the continued murmuring sound of falling water, which runs through the square tube (fig. 17) in the left side of the cave and falls into one of the bottomless pits. This hall is from seven to twelve feet in height above the clay which fills the lower portion of the cave, and which, when washed out, will reveal one of the rooms well calculated to excite wonder and admiration. The walls are more or less water-worn and even. A stream of water flows on the right, which is crossed near the middle of the hall. Near the further end of this hall, the cave widens on the right side and terminates rather abruptly, the passage being on the extreme left. From the right, in the corner of the wide portion of the cave, a side cave (fig. 18) passes to the distance of several rods, where it becomes filled with clay. On passing into the narrow portion of the cave, on the left, we come to the

POOL OF SILOAM (Fig. 19),

Which is from seven to twelve feet in height and width. The sides and top are water-worn and often smooth. A stream of water flows on the left. Here we find ourselves among arches and cavities of almost every size and description, and which are likened to almost everything. The guides point out the Giant's Spectacles, the Iron Kettle and the Wash Basin, while neighbor plowman sees the exact imprint of the face and horns of his favorite ox, the one he has so often driven o'er the lea, and Lady Lynx-eye finds a dozen figures in pantomime.

On leaving the Pool of Siloam we come to

THE INDIAN STONE LADDER (Fig. 20),

Which consists of some well laid stone steps which lead to the top of a hill of rocks, where, on our left, on looking over a low stone wall, we find a pit (fig. 21) five or six feet in width and about twelve feet in length, which the guides tell you has no lower end. This pit seems to consist of a portion of rock separated by fracture, and gone where? Into a giant cave below. Here, with lamp in hand, the visitor will often gaze over the wall into the depths of impenetrable darkness, and wonder and ask if it is really bottomless, and, perhaps, now, for the first in life, realize the danger of the pit with no bottom.

Turning now to the right hand side of the main cave, we find a cave (fig. 22) leaving the main cave at right angles. This cave is about three feet high at its entrance, but increases in height as it goes in.

After advancing four or five rods we come to some large stalactitic formations, one of which is six feet in diameter and twenty feet in height, and which is strangely broken off and displaced, called by the guides the Tower of Babel (fig. 23). This cave is probably the extreme upper portion of a high cave, the bottom being filled with clay, the top of which forms the path.

Retracing our steps to the main cave, we pass down the hill at the foot of which we find

FRANKLIN AVENUE (FIG. 24).

Turning now to our left, we find a cave (fig. 25) leading to the further end of the bottomless pit, near which it is now obstructed by a wall, except for the passage of water.

This avenue, we are told by the guides, was once the residence of FRANKLIN, and that this world can boast of its celebrities as well as the world above. This avenue presents a great variety of views. The walls are often water-worn smooth but not even. One person sees port-holes, shot-holes, &c., and likens it to the inside of some ship of war, while another person sees cradles, milk-pans and demijohns, all of which are in the arch of the Cave, and of course empty ; but the guides inform you with much gravity, that when the earth rolls over, all these utensils will be right side up. The guides point out William Penn's monument, hat, &c.

Near the further end of this avenue we find a large stalagmite (fig. 26) six or seven feet in diameter, which just fills a cave, except in height. This cave is probably the upper portion of a high cave which is now almost completely obstructed by clay, and the depth of the stalagmite below the path is not known.

On passing this stalagmite, we ascend some steps which land us in the next department, which is

FLOOD HALL (FIG. 27).

This hall is from eight to twelve feet in height and width. The walls are not very even, and the clay is of an undetermined depth.

On leaving this we come to

CONGRESS HALL (Fig. 28),

Where the Cave is from twelve to eighteen feet in height and width. The walls are generally even and often water-worn smooth. The stream flows first on the right and then on the left. Almost the whole of this room is well adapted for public speaking.

Here, for the first, sounds reflect so as to become musical. Here, for the first, the visitor often thoughtlessly begins his musical strains, and gazing and stopping, and marching to the tune, he at length arrives at the further end of the hall where the Cave widens on the right, which is called the

GHOST ROOM, OR HAUNTED CASTLE (Fig. 29).

This room is upon a clay bank which is probably from ten to twenty feet deep.

At the right-hand corner we find a branch cave (fig. 30), which is of some interest, as it shows the decomposition of the rock in a striking manner. This room, like the hall we have passed, is musical, but has that peculiar formation which fits it for the reflection of sound from and to certain places with peculiar force, and to some extent from all places. Let a person place himself in one of the niches (fig. 31) and utter sounds while the listener is standing in front, and he will find difficulty in telling its source, while if he steps a little to the right the sound appears to proceed from overhead.

Here the visitor often calls and listens for departed spirits; here he invokes the gods to listen to his wants; but here, as in the upper world, the prayers of the faithless are heeded not.

Having now become slightly acquainted with reflected and musical sounds, let us proceeed to the next department, which is

MUSIC HALL (Fig. 32),

Where every sound is music, and where he now sings who never sung before, and who after leaving never utters more.

This hall is from twenty to thirty feet in width, and from fifteen to twenty-five in height. The floor is level and even till near the further end, where it becomes somewhat rocky. The sides and especially the arch, present a great variety of cavities and smooth, contorted surfaces which front in all directions, and which seems to favor the reflection of sound. A pistol fired in this hall sounds like a heavy piece of artillery, and reverberates a long time.

Near the further end we find two large stalagmites on the right (fig. 33), which are from ten to twelve feet in diameter, and near by a naturally formed column of cement rock, which seems to support a world of rock above.

A small stream meanders along the whole length of this hall, which has its fountain in the

STYGIAN LAKE (Fig. 34).

This lake is nearly one-fourth of a mile in length, and is scarcely less in size or less musical than the room we have just passed, but all else how changed.

The rocky terra firma has here given way to a long deep sheet of water, and our pedestrian pilgrimage has changed to boating.

The smooth water-worn contorted surfaces of Music Hall have disappeared, and the roof and the rocky walls are now draped with stalactites which assume a thousand different forms, and in which a person of even a slightly imaginative turn of mind, can find not only the prototype of the whole vegetable and animal world in whole and in parts, but the works of art included.

The water is from two to sixteen feet deep, and is remarkable for its transparency, the bottom being plainly seen by lamp light even where several feet deep.

This lake is crossed by a boat of sufficient capacity to carry ten or twelve persons with convenience, and twenty or more persons may ride with safety and but little inconvenience.

The boat lying now in wait, let us embark for Plymouth Rock (fig.35), and as we pass ever and anon stop and gaze and wonder. Just ahead on the right, the guides point out a larger stalactite hanging from the roof called the Harp, which belongs to the Lady of the Lake, and which on being gently struck with a stick, emits musical sounds, which vary according to the place struck. On our right we find high clay banks, which are often covered with stalactitic formations.

Near the center of the lake on the left, we are shown a stalagmite called the Lady of the Lake, and near the further end a large stalagmite on the right called the Church Organ.

Just beyond this we come to the wharf which leads directly to

PLYMOUTH ROCK (Fig. 35),

Where we soon find our passage obstructed by a large stalagmite (fig. 36), which, not satisfied to just fill the cave from top to bottom, it extends in its length.

Upon this stalagmite, as upon many other parts of the cave, we find the initials of many a visitor chiseled on marble.

Turning now to our left we come to a ladder by which we ascend about eight feet, to the threshold of

THE DEVIL'S GANGWAY (Fig. 37).

This gangway is a cave about three feet in diameter, passing around the large stalagmite, and enters the main cave beyond, where we come to

THE MUSEUM (Fig. 38).

This room is from eighteen to twenty feet in height and width. The Stygian river flows first on the right and then on the left.

This museum has a liberal supply of specimens, and although more ancient than Barnum's, is still deficient in one specimen, for which the whole cave empire has been searched in vain, a specimen which plays so important a part in the affairs of the upper world, and flourishes only in barren soils where needed. This specimen is called Humbug.

On leaving this room at the foot of a hill we come to

THE GEOLOGICAL ROOMS (Fig. 39).

This room is generally higher and wider than the room we have just passed, and the top is generally more even and studded with stalagmites. A large part of this room has a floor of stiff clay, the depth of which I have no very definite idea. The next room we come to is

UNCLE TOM'S CABIN (Fig. 40),

Which is a short expansion of the Cave in height and width for less than a hundred feet, and, although unimportant in size, nature has here engraved in bas-relief one of the most important events in the history of the upper world, which consists of Uncle Tom and his funeral attendants in procession. So say the guides.

On leaving this room we come to

THE GIANT'S STUDY (Fig. 41),

In which the arch of the Cave is rather more elevated than the room we have just passed, but the floor is more rocky and uneven. Here we find some large rocks rather strangely arranged by the hand of nature, one of which is called, by the guides, the Speaker's Stand, another the Writing Table, another the Book, in which is recorded the history of the Cave, and all things connected with it, and when we take into consideration that it is a specimen of a strata in which there is entombed more than a hundred different petrifications, we find some truth in the assertion of the guides, whether so intended or not.

From this we pass into

GIANT'S NURSERY (Fig. 42),

Which is from ten to sixteen feet in height and width. Here the guides point out tables, bathing-tubs and cradles, in short, a copious supply of implements suited to this department, nearly all of which are in the arch of the cave. From this we pass into

THE PIRATE'S CAVE (Fig. 43),

Which commences at the large stalagmite on the left, called

by the guides the Hottentot's Tent, with the juveniles playing on the top; the juveniles being the small stalagmites on the large one. This room extends to the foot of the Rocky Mountains, and contains many arches and columns formed of the natural rock. A stream of water flows on the left, which is crossed at the foot of

THE ROCKY MOUNTAINS (Fig. 44).

Which is the next place on our line of march.

These mountains afford the most wonderful scenery to be found in the whole subterranean world. Here we find piles upon piles of gigantic rock thrown together in the most promiscuous manner.

Here we find stalagmites, the growth of eternal centuries, broken and sharing in the common confusion. Here one is forced to doubt the truth of the assertion of Pope, where he says,

> Order is heaven's first law.

On climbing up these mountains we come to a large broken stalagmite called the Leaning Tower of Pisa, of which the one at Pisa is a very perfect imitation. On advancing a little further we come to some large stalagmites on the left, which are from twelve to sixteen feet in diameter, and whose base is supposed to be on the same plane as the mountains above whose pinnacle they tower. One of these is called the Elephant's Back, and which is often a resting place for the weary pilgrim.

Here the Bloomers often request the animal to go, but he don't; they urge him to go, but he don't; they command him to go, but he, like some of his riders, the more he's urged the more he won't, so our pedestrian journey must be resumed, and on traveling a short distance we halt a moment, when, lo! our whole heavens are at once lighted up by the red light which extends our vision distinctly into all the regions of space, both in the heavens above and in the mountains around, and which can only be appreciated by being seen. After passing a few rods we come to what the guides call the Mermaid, which seems to be strangely out of place. A pilgrim probably.

On passing down the mountains, we go under and between a huge pile of rocks (fig. 45), which are wedged in between the sides of the Cave, at the foot of which we come to one low, short place where (humiliating as it may be) the upper tens must decidedly bow.

On passing this low, narrow place, we come to a department which bears the name of one who reigned almost three thousand years ago, which is

THE VALLEY OF JEHOSAPHAT (Fig. 46).

This valley is from eight to twelve feet in width, and in height one is forced to think of the pine-tree tops told of by Tupper, or some one, who says, too high to be seen except by the stars. Along our left, high up in the region of darkness, may be seen a kind of projecting rock called the Table Rock, which is accessible over and through the detached mass of rock in the mountains we have just passed; but this is never visited except by those of the Blondin type. The floor is full of rocks, which are unevenly distributed; sometimes you rise some sharp pinnacle, then go to the extreme left or right, then down or across the stream which meanders among the rocks for the whole distance, which is over one-fourth of a mile.

In this valley may be seen fragments of large stalagmites, which some unknown force has broken and distributed in various places, and the corroding action of the water in destroying them is plainly to be seen.

This valley terminates where the Cave divides into three divisions; the right-hand division, being the most interesting division, is next to be noticed, and is called

THE WINDING WAY (Fig. 47).

The arrow indicates its direction from the main cave.

Here again, more than ever, it seems that nature is exhaustless in the variety and grandeur of her works; here the scenery is entirely unlike anything we have heretofore seen. Separate the skull bones of an animal where it is joined by sutures, and you get an idea of the ground view of its windings. In width it is from two to four feet, and in height from three to twenty feet. The walls are often covered with stalactitic formations, most of which are perfectly white or translucent. Here we find a few bridges of stalactitic formation. In length it is about one-fourth of a mile. After having passed about two-thirds the distance, we come to where a large triangular rock is broken out on the right hand side, and gone perhaps thirty feet below the clay path on which you walk. The large cavity thus formed is called the Sitting Room (fig. 48), where we all take a rest and chat about the wonders of the past journey, each calling to mind something peculiar which had escaped the notice of all the rest. Here we all blow out our lights, and at once appreciate darkness. Here we all try to keep perfectly still one whole minute, and find it a long period of silence. Here the muscular system often begins to cave in. Here is the place where the back track is usually taken.

On pursuing our course to the end of Winding Way, we find, low down on the right, a round hole (fig. 49), about the size of a barrel, which enlarges after a few feet and leads to

THE ROTUNDA (Fig. 50),

Which consists of a high, round chamber, the height of which has never been measured.

GENERAL REMARKS.

There is good reason to believe that the water-worn rock bottom of this cave is not to be seen for more than one-twentieth of the whole distance traveled, the lower portion being filled with clay, which is sometimes mixed with stones of various sizes. In many places clay banks may be seen extending up either one or both sides of the cave, sometimes to the height of eighteen feet.

Generally we have no means of ascertaining the depth of these clay deposits, but that it is over thirty feet deep in some places is almost certain. Frequently we see the stream, which runs along close to the side of the cave, wash away the clay ten feet below the path on which you walk, without any sign of a rock bottom. So that generally it may be considered that in walking through this cave we are near its upper portion. In a few places we pass where the bottom seems to consist of loose rock which fell centuries ago from the arch of the cave, and which now give it that pointed form of the arch which, at first sight, seems to bid defiance to any further destruction by the hand of time.

The branch or side caves are, with few exceptions, more or less filled with clay, and it is probable that some of the branch caves are, in reality, larger than the main cave is above the clay which fills the lower portion. In fact, there is good reason to believe, that what are now called branch caves are, in reality, much the oldest.

From a general view of Winding Way and its junction, with the high valley of Jehosaphat, there is good reason to believe that its real rock bottom is at least twenty feet below the clay path.

There are several branch caves which are almost completely filled with clay, which are not noted in the illustration, and it is probable that many more will be discovered as the clay is washed out of the sides by the floods of spring, and as the clay which fills the lower portion is removed, it is probable that they will increase both in size and number.

There are no fish in the waters of this Cave, except such as have been carried there for a new abode, and which are said to flourish for a season, but leave during the floods of spring for a climate more congenial to their nature.

During the fall and winter months large numbers of bats resort here to hibernate and, like SHAKSPEARE'S toad, to fatten on the vapors of a dungeon, till the warmth of spring in the upper world is suited to their wants.

They may often be seen hanging to the side of the Cave in clusters of several dozen, each clinging to his neighbor like bees at the time of swarming.

In some places there are small patches of mud which

swarm with the common fish-worm which seems to be acclimated here.

This Cave does not abound in the bones of animals; only one skeleton was ever found more than a mile from its entrance, and this the bones of a bear, which were procured for the Smithsonian Institution at Washington.

www.ingramcontent.com/pod-product-compliance
Lightning Source LLC
LaVergne TN
LVHW010743120826
845150LV00009B/2284

* 9 7 8 1 4 1 8 1 9 4 7 1 0 *